First published in the United States by
The Lighthouse Academy Press
Printed by Kindle Direct Publishing, USA
Additional copies for sale at Amazon Books

ISBN: 979-8-9953537-4-4

This work was created through a human–AI collaboration.
The author directed, revised, and finalized all content.
See *Author's Note.*

Standing Before Homer

Restoring the Way
The Iliad and The Odyssey
Were Meant to Be Heard

William J. Striker

Contents

Author's Note

This book arises from a simple observation: *The Iliad* and *The Odyssey* are widely read, yet they are rarely received as they once were.

The change is not in the poems themselves. It is in the position of the reader. Over time, the manner of approach has shifted — from participation to observation, from recognition to interpretation. That shift has brought clarity, but it has also introduced distance. What was once encountered as conduct under pressure is now often approached as material for explanation.

This work was written to make that difference visible.

It does not attempt to replace modern understanding, nor to argue against it. The aim is narrower: to restore a prior position from which these works may first be encountered as they were meant to be — before analysis, before abstraction, before the impulse to explain. From that position, much that now appears distant may become immediate again.

A word is appropriate regarding authorship.

This work was developed with the assistance of modern artificial intelligence tools. These tools were used as instruments of exploration — to test structure, refine phrasing, and examine the clarity of expression. They contributed to drafting in part, but not to judgment. The ordering of the material, the selection of what to include and what to leave aside, the interpretation of the poems, and the final form of every passage remain the responsibility of the author.

Artificial intelligence does not think. It does not stand within a point of view, nor does it judge from within experience. It produces outputs through learned patterns applied to input. That capacity can assist in shaping language, but it does not constitute authorship.

Authorship requires judgment. For that reason, this book should be read as a human work that is assisted in its formation, but directed, weighed, and completed by a single voice.

The reader is invited to meet it in that spirit.

Preface

These works are widely read. They are rarely received.

They have passed through many hands — sung, written, copied, translated, analyzed. Each age has approached them in its own way and, not without reason, found in them something that corresponds to its own condition. There are gains in this. There is clarity, method, and precision. There is also loss — less visible, but no less real.

The greatest change has not been in the works themselves. It has been in the position of the one who receives them.

Where the first listeners stood within the story, the modern reader stands apart from it. Where they heard conduct under pressure, we are inclined to seek explanation. Where action carried immediate consequence, we often encounter abstraction. These are not errors so much as the natural posture of a different world.

This book does not set out to correct that posture by argument. It seeks instead to make it visible.

To understand these works, one must resist the urge to interpret them at once. One must first learn to stand, as nearly as possible, where their first listeners stood — to see what they saw, to notice what they noticed, and to recognize what required no explanation. This is not an attempt to return to the past, but to recover a position from which certain things become easier to see.

The Greeks had a word for the proper way to receive a stranger: *xenia*. The stranger was not questioned immediately, nor judged, nor explained. He was first received — given place, offered food, and treated with respect. Only then did conversation begin.

The same discipline is required of the reader.

A work such as this cannot be interrogated at once. It must first be received. The task of the host is to prepare the ground — to order the encounter so that what is present may be seen without distortion. The task of the guest is no less important: to enter with attentiveness, to restrain premature judgment, and to allow what is there to emerge in its own sequence.

This is not a relation of expert and student. It is a meeting of host and guest. Each has a role to fulfill. If either neglects it, the encounter fails.

What follows is not an explanation of these works, nor an argument about what they mean. It is an attempt to restore the conditions under which they can be properly received. If those conditions are established, much that now appears distant or obscure may become immediate again — not through effort, but through position.

These works were not created to be studied in the modern sense. They were created to shape those who heard them. They do so still, when they are encountered as they were meant to be.

The reader is not asked to abandon what he knows, but to stand for a time in a different place — and to notice what appears there.

Standing Before Homer

Part I:
The Position of the Reader

Chapter 1
Where You Stand Determines
What You See

A work does not present itself in the same way to every reader. What is seen depends first on where one stands. This is not a matter of opinion or preference. It is a matter of position. The same words may be read; the same scenes encountered; the same actions described. Yet what is recognized within them will differ, sometimes sharply, according to the posture of the one who receives them. A reader may approach a work as an object to be examined, or as an encounter to be entered. He may stand outside it, or within it. The difference is decisive.

In the modern habit, a work is most often approached from a distance. It is taken up, considered, and set before the mind as something to be understood. Questions arise quickly: what does it mean, what does it represent, what does it reveal about its time or its author? These questions are not without value; they bring clarity and order. But they also introduce a separation. The work is placed at arm's length, and the reader stands apart from it.

In another posture, older and now less familiar, the work is not first examined. It is received. The distinction is quiet, but it governs everything that follows.

To receive a work is not to abandon thought. It is to delay it. It is to allow what is present to appear before it is explained. Attention comes first; interpretation follows, if it is still required. The reader does not begin by asking what the work means. He begins by observing what is done, what is said, and what is borne. This shift is small in description. In practice, it alters the entire field of perception.

Consider two readers approaching the same scene. A man stands before danger. One reader asks: what does this signify, what theme is being expressed, what idea is illustrated? The other asks nothing at first. He watches. He notices how the man speaks, how he moves, what he refuses, what he accepts. He sees not a symbol, but a pattern of conduct.

The first reader will arrive at an interpretation. The second will recognize something more immediate. Neither is necessarily in error. But they do not see the same thing.

In the works attributed to Homer, this difference becomes especially clear. These works emerged in a world where life was not encountered at a distance. Risk was not abstract, nor was consequence deferred. Action and result were closely joined, and reputation was not a matter of preference but of survival. In such a world, a story was not an object of study. It was a presentation of conduct under conditions that were widely understood.

The listener did not need to be told what was at stake. He knew. He did not need to be instructed in what to admire or condemn. He recognized it. This does not mean that the ancient listener was simpler, nor that the modern reader is more sophisticated. Each stands within the conditions of his own age, and each brings with him the habits those conditions have formed. The modern reader possesses forms of clarity that were not available before: historical awareness, analytical method, a capacity to compare and to distinguish. These are real gains. But they are not without cost.

When a work is approached primarily as something to be understood, it is easily removed from the conditions that gave it weight. Action becomes example. Speech becomes expression. Consequence becomes theme. The reader gains clarity, but loses immediacy. He sees more precisely, but feels less directly what is at stake. This is not a fault. It is a development. It is also a narrowing. To see only what can be explained is to see less than what is there.

The purpose of this chapter is not to reject the modern posture, nor to replace it with another. It is to make the difference visible. Once seen, it cannot be entirely forgotten, and the reader may choose, at times, to stand elsewhere.

These ancient works do not require belief, nor do they demand agreement. They ask only for attention. They present actions, decisions, and consequences without explanation, and they allow the reader to observe what holds and what fails under pressure.

To approach them well, one must be willing to suspend certain habits. Not permanently, and not completely. But long enough to see what appears when they are set aside. This requires a kind of restraint that is no longer common in reading. The impulse to interpret is strong; it gives a sense of progress and control. But it can also prevent something simpler from occurring: the recognition of what is plainly before us.

A man speaks.

Another responds.

A choice is made.

A consequence follows.

Nothing is hidden. Nothing is encoded. And yet, without the proper position, much of it is missed.

The reader who stands apart may still understand the work. He may describe it accurately, analyze it effectively, and relate it to other works and ideas. But he will have encountered it as something observed, not as something entered.

The reader who stands within it will see something else. He will not see more in quantity, but differently in kind. He will see how a man carries himself when he cannot escape what is before him. He will see how speech binds, how action reveals, and how consequence settles without appeal. He will recognize patterns that do not require explanation, because they correspond to conditions that, in another form, still remain.

This is the position from which these works were first heard. It is not beyond recovery. It requires only that the reader stand, for a time, where the explanation has not yet begun — and attend to what is there. From that position, much that appears distant becomes near. And what is near, once seen clearly, does not require interpretation to be understood.

Chapter 2
The World of the First Listeners

The works attributed to Homer did not first appear as texts. They were heard. They were spoken in a world where life was not arranged at a distance. What was said was bound to what was done; what was done carried consequence without delay. The listener did not enter the story from a place of safety. He stood within conditions that resembled those presented before him.

This is the first difference that must be made clear.

The modern reader is accustomed to a degree of separation. Events may be observed, considered, and set aside. Risk is often mediated; consequence is frequently deferred. One may examine an action without being subject to its result. This produces clarity, but it also permits a certain detachment.

The early listener did not possess this distance in the same way. He lived within a narrow margin. The day's work was not optional, and its failure was not easily absorbed. Travel exposed a man to uncertainty; the sea did not forgive error, and the land beyond one's own could not be assumed to receive a stranger well. A household depended on its order; a disruption within it did not remain contained. These were not exceptional conditions. They were the ordinary frame of life.

Within such a frame, conduct was not a matter of expression. It was a matter of survival. A man's standing was not held internally. It was carried in the regard of others. Reputation did not follow action at a distance; it accompanied it. To be known as reliable, measured, or reckless was not a description. It was a condition that shaped how one was received, trusted, or opposed. A word given could not be lightly withdrawn; to do so altered the man who spoke it in the eyes of those who heard.

Speech, therefore, was not separate from action. It was a form of it. When a man declared his intent, he did not describe a possibility. He established a line from which departure would be visible and judged. Silence, too, had weight. To refrain from speaking in a moment that called for it was itself a kind of statement. In such a world, nothing that was said could be treated as merely expressive.

This extends to the structure of the household. The house was not only a place of residence. It was the center of order. Those who belonged to it were bound by roles that were understood without explanation. The arrival of a stranger introduced both risk and obligation. To receive him properly required resources and discipline; to refuse him without cause could mark the host as deficient. The practice known as hospitality was not courtesy. It was a test of whether order could be maintained in the presence of the unknown. Failure in this regard did not remain local. It signaled something about the man and the house, and that signal carried outward.

From this, a pattern becomes visible. Conduct is always seen in relation to conditions. It is not abstracted from them, nor evaluated apart from their pressures. A man is not judged by what he intends, but by how he carries himself when intention meets resistance.

The Iliad and *The Odyssey* present such moments without interruption.

A choice is made.

A word is spoken.

An action is taken.

The consequence arrives.

There is little delay, and less explanation. The listener is not guided toward a conclusion. He is shown what holds and what fails when tested.

This is especially clear in the treatment of conflict. Conflict is not introduced as a problem to be solved. It is given as a condition to be met. A man may avoid it, or he may enter it; he may bear it well, or poorly. But once it is present, it does not wait upon interpretation. It requires response.

Death, in this setting, is neither distant nor rare. It does not require framing. Its presence shapes the scale of all other considerations. A decision made under such a condition carries a weight that is immediately understood. The listener does not need to be reminded of what is at stake. He already knows. This knowledge does not produce uniform behavior. It does not guarantee restraint or wisdom. It does, however, establish a field in which actions are measured against consequence without mediation. What a man does is not separated from what follows.

From within such a field, the events of these works do not appear as symbolic or exaggerated. They appear as intensified presentations of conditions that are already familiar.

A man refuses an obligation.

Another responds.

The situation escalates.

The outcome settles the matter.

Nothing in this sequence requires interpretation. It requires only recognition.

The same is true of endurance. To persist under difficulty is not presented as admirable in itself. It is expected. The question is not whether a man will endure, but how he will do so. Will he maintain proportion, or will he give way to excess? Will he remain aligned with himself, or will he depart from what he has already established? These are not questions asked in the text. They are answered in action. For the listener, the answer is not received as an idea. It is seen in the manner of the man.

This is the world in which these works were first heard. It does not need to be reconstructed in detail. It needs only to be recognized in outline. Life is immediate. Speech binds. Reputation is visible. Consequence follows. Within such a setting, nothing that occurs is abstract.

If the reader is able to stand, even briefly, within these conditions, much that appears distant will begin to take on a different weight. Actions that seemed excessive may appear proportioned to the circumstances. Restraint that seemed unnecessary may reveal its necessity. What once required explanation may no longer need it.

The conditions need not be held. It is sufficient that they are seen.

From this point forward, the poems themselves provide the rest.

Chapter 3
Xenia: How to Receive a Stranger

There was a word for the proper way to receive a stranger. It did not refer to courtesy. It referred to order.

Xenia named a structure within which the unknown could be admitted without dissolving the house. It governed what was to be done when a man appeared at the threshold: how he was to be received, how he was to be treated, and how he, in turn, was to conduct himself once received.

The sequence was fixed. The stranger was not questioned at once. He was given place. Food was set before him. His condition was restored before his identity was examined. Only then did speech begin. This was not generosity alone. It was discipline.

To question too early was to place curiosity above order. To refuse the stranger outright was to risk hardness. To admit him without measure was to invite disorder into the house. The practice held these tensions in balance. It allowed the unknown to be encountered without surrendering the structure that made the encounter possible.

The responsibility did not rest with the host alone. The guest was also bound. He was to accept what was offered without presumption. He was to speak when it was proper, not when it pleased him. He was not to take more than was given, nor to remain beyond his place. He entered under protection, but not without obligation. If he failed in this, the protection was withdrawn, and the failure did not remain private. It marked him.

The relation was reciprocal. It depended on proportion from both sides. If either failed, the result was not discomfort. It was disorder. This is made clear not by instruction, but by contrast.

In *The Odyssey*, there are houses in which this order is maintained. The stranger is received, restored, and then known. The exchange proceeds within limits that are understood without being stated. Nothing remarkable occurs. That is the point. Order holds.

There is also a house in which this order has broken. The men who occupy it do not receive; they consume. They do not wait; they take. They do not measure themselves; they exceed. What is given for sustenance is taken for pleasure; what is offered for a time is held without end. They speak without restraint and act without proportion. They are not merely impolite. They have placed themselves outside the structure that permits men to live together without constant conflict. The consequence follows.

This pattern does not need to be explained to the listener. It is visible in the conduct itself. Where proportion is maintained, order persists. Where it is abandoned, disorder spreads and must be corrected.

The same structure governs the encounter between reader and text. A work such as *The Iliad* or *The Odyssey* is not an object to be taken up at once and made to yield its meaning. It stands, as the stranger once stood, at the threshold. It must be received before it is questioned.

This does not diminish the reader. It assigns him a role. He must allow the work to present itself in its own order. He must resist the impulse to ask at once what it signifies, what it represents, or how it may be used. He must attend to what is said and done, and to the sequence in which it appears. He must accept what is given before seeking to take more. This requires restraint. The modern habit inclines otherwise. The reader is trained to approach a work with questions prepared. He seeks orientation immediately, and often receives it. Summaries are provided, themes are identified, meanings are suggested. The encounter is ordered in advance.

Something is gained in this. Much is clarified quickly. Something is also lost. The work is not allowed to stand in its own form. It is entered already explained. The reader is not required to attend with care, because the path has been set before him. He moves through the work with direction, but without discovery. In terms of the older practice, this is a failure of reception. It is not an offense of intent. It is a departure from sequence.

To receive properly, the reader must accept a different order. He must begin without question. This does not mean that questions are forbidden. It means that they are not first. They follow, if they remain necessary, after the work has been allowed to appear.

The reader must also accept limits. He cannot take from the work whatever he wishes at any moment. He must proceed as it proceeds. He must remain within the boundaries it establishes. He must not impose upon it a structure that belongs to him rather than to it. This, too, is a form of discipline. It does not constrain understanding. It makes it possible. Within this discipline, the encounter becomes reciprocal. The work offers itself in action, speech, and consequence. The reader offers attention, patience, and restraint. Neither dominates. Neither withdraws. Each fulfills a role that permits the other to be present without distortion.

If the reader fails in this, the work does not disappear. It remains. But it is not properly seen. Its parts may be described, its structure analyzed, its themes identified. Yet what is most immediate within it will have been missed. This is not a failure of intelligence. It is a failure of reception.

The correction does not require effort so much as sequence.

Receive first.

Then consider.

The practice is simple. It is also exacting. It places a demand upon the reader that is no longer commonly made: that he enter without taking, attend without imposing, and allow what is present to emerge before he names it.

In return, the work yields what cannot be forced. It shows, without instruction, what holds and what fails when a man is placed under pressure. It presents conduct in its relation to consequence, without mediation. It allows recognition to occur without being guided toward it.

This is the exchange that *xenia* made possible between men. It remains possible between the reader and the work. The structure has not changed. Only the habit of observing it has weakened. It may be restored.

Nothing more is required than that the reader accept the role that has always been his: to stand at the threshold, to enter in order, and to receive what is there before asking what it means.

Chapter 4
How the Reader Was Moved —
and Moved Away

The works themselves have not changed. They have been sung, written, copied, translated, and studied. Their language has been carried across centuries; their scenes remain what they were. A man stands before danger; another refuses; a third endures; a fourth fails. The actions are the same.

What has changed is the position from which they are received. This change did not occur at once. It took place gradually, through a series of shifts that altered not the works, but the habits brought to them. The movement was not directed toward loss, nor was it without gain. It followed the conditions of each age, and it answered to them.

To see it clearly, one must observe not the text, but the reader.

The First Movement — From Hearing to Holding

When these works were first heard, they existed within performance. They were carried by voice, received by ear, and held in memory. The listener did not possess the work; he participated in it. It unfolded in time and passed, leaving behind not a fixed object but an impression shaped by attention and recall.

When the poems eventually entered written form, something changed. They could now be held. They could be returned to, compared, and preserved without reliance on memory alone. The sequence of events became stable; the wording could be examined. The work no longer depended entirely on the presence of the speaker or the readiness of the listener. This was a gain. It allowed for continuity. It protected the work from loss. It made possible a more exact engagement with what was said. But it also introduced a new relation. The work could now be approached as something that existed apart from the moment of its reception. It could be taken up at will, entered at any point, and revisited without limit. The reader began to stand not only within the work, but also apart from it.

The change was small at first. The habits of the earlier world remained. The written form did not immediately produce a different posture. But the conditions for such a change had been established.

The Second Movement — From Participation to Reflection

As thought turned increasingly toward its own processes, the works were no longer only received. They were considered. By the classical period in Greece, in the 5th and 4th centuries BC, this reflective posture had become explicit. Writers such as Plato and Aristotle did not treat these works as neutral. They understood them to have an effect upon those who encountered them. They asked what kind of character was formed by what was heard, and they did not assume that the effect was always beneficial. This, too, was a gain. It brought attention to the shaping power of the work. It made explicit what had previously been implicit. It introduced a discipline of thought that could examine not only what was presented, but what it produced. Yet even here, the works were not set at a distance in the modern sense. They remained within the field of formation. The question was not merely what they meant, but what they did to a man.

The reader began to reflect upon the work, but he had not yet withdrawn from it.

The Third Movement — From Formation to Preservation

As these works passed into the care of later cultures, they were preserved under new conditions. In the centuries that followed, as these works passed through Greek, Roman, and later European institutions of preservation, they were copied, studied, and transmitted within institutions that did not share the original setting of their composition. The language in which they were written was no longer commonly spoken; the world they depicted was no longer directly known. They were retained because they were judged to be of value.

That value was often expressed in moral or exemplary terms. The works were read for what they could teach, for the patterns they displayed, and for the order they were thought to contain. They were placed alongside other texts that served similar purposes, and they were approached within a framework that sought alignment with a broader understanding of life. This preserved them. It also reframed them. The reader was now more clearly separated from the conditions within which the works had first been heard. He approached them through mediation: through language, through commentary, through a setting that was not their own. The posture shifted again.

The works were still formative, but they were now received through a layer of interpretation that stood between the reader and the action itself.

The Fourth Movement — From Reflection to Analysis

With the rise of modern philology, especially from the late eighteenth century onward, the relation changed more sharply. The work became an object of study. Questions were asked concerning its origin, its composition, its sources, and its structure. The language was examined in detail; variants were compared; historical conditions were reconstructed. The work was situated within a broader field of knowledge, and it was approached with methods designed to produce clarity and precision. This, again, was a gain. Much that had been uncertain became clearer. The form of the work could be understood with greater exactness. Its relation to other works and traditions could be traced. The reader was no longer dependent upon inheritance alone; he could investigate. But this clarity came with a cost. The work was now held at a distance. It was approached as something to be known, rather than something within which one stood. The reader's attention was directed toward explanation, and the sequence of the work was often reordered to serve that aim. Summary replaced unfolding; interpretation accompanied or preceded observation.

The posture had shifted from participation to analysis.

The Present Condition

The modern reader, shaped by these centuries of development, inherits all of these movements. He has access to the text in stable form. He can return to it at will. He is aware of its history, its language, and its place within a larger tradition. He has at his disposal methods of interpretation that bring clarity and distinction. He also stands at a distance. The work is available to him, but it does not require him. He may approach it when he chooses, and he may leave it without consequence. He may enter with questions already formed, and he may receive answers without attending to the order in which they arise.

This condition is not deficient. It is the result of developments that have brought real advantages. It is also incomplete. For in gaining the ability to explain, the reader has, in part, lost the necessity to attend. In gaining access, he has lost immediacy. In gaining clarity, he has accepted a degree of separation. He sees more, but not always what is most direct.

What Has Been Moved Away

The earlier posture did not exclude thought. It placed thought in sequence. The modern posture does not exclude recognition, but it often places explanation before it. The difference is not in the capacity of the reader, but in the order of his engagement. When explanation comes first, it shapes what is seen. When observation comes first, it allows what is present to appear before it is named.

This is the difference that has been introduced. It need not be accepted without remainder.

Restoring Position Without Rejecting Gain

The movements described are not to be undone. They cannot be set aside entirely, nor would it be desirable to do so. The clarity that has been gained is real, and it serves.

The task is not to return to an earlier condition. It is to restore a position within the present one. The reader may retain what has been gained — his ability to distinguish, to compare, to understand structure and context. But he may also choose, at the outset of his encounter, to suspend these operations long enough to allow the work to appear in its own order.

He may receive before he analyzes. This is not a rejection. It is a reordering.

The Simple Correction

Nothing more is required than a change in sequence. The work is taken up. It is allowed to unfold. Attention is given to what is said and done, and to the order in which it appears. Only after this has occurred does the reader return, if he wishes, to consider, to compare, and to explain.

In this way, what has been gained is not lost, and what has been set aside is not forgotten. The reader stands, for a time, where the first listeners stood. He is then free to move. But he does not begin there.

The poems have not moved. The reader has. He need only take a step back — and observe.

Part II:
The Iliad: How a Man Faces Death

Chapter 5
Not About War, But About Bearing

The work commonly called *The Iliad* is set in war. This is evident from the first lines. Armies are gathered. Alliances are named. Weapons are taken up. Men are placed in opposition, and the conditions of conflict are established without delay.

From this, a conclusion is often drawn: that the work is about war. It is not. War is the condition within which the action occurs. It is not the subject. The distinction matters.

War, in this setting, is not presented as a problem to be solved or a circumstance to be explained. It is given as a fact. It is already underway when the work begins, and it remains unresolved when it ends. No strategy is proposed that would bring it to a close; no judgment is offered that would place it within a larger argument. The work does not ask whether the war is justified. It asks how a man conducts himself within it.

The opening movement is not a battle. It is a refusal. Achilles withdraws. He does not leave the field entirely. He remains present, but he refuses to act. He declines to fight, to lead, or to contribute to the effort in which he has been placed. The reason is stated; the cause is clear.

A dispute has arisen, and he will not accept the terms imposed upon him. The consequence follows. The army suffers. This sequence is not presented as an argument. It is not explained in terms of policy or principle. It is shown. There is no interior account of what a man thinks. His reasons are not set out before the reader. His doubts are not explained. What he carries appears only in what he does.

The reader is not told why the man acts. He sees what follows from it.

A man refuses.

Others bear the result.

No further instruction is given. The reader may be inclined to ask whether Achilles is right. We are offered no answer. Instead we are presented with what occurs when his decision meets the conditions in which it is made. The refusal does not remain contained within the man who makes it. It extends outward. It alters the balance of the field. It exposes others to what he has chosen not to bear.

This pattern appears. Action, or the absence of it, does not remain private.

The work proceeds in this manner. A man stands before danger. He advances, or he hesitates. He speaks, or he remains silent. Each choice carries forward into consequence. Nothing is isolated. Nothing is without effect.

The field of war makes this visible without delay. Where consequence might otherwise be deferred, here it is immediate. Where failure might be absorbed, here it is final. The scale is not enlarged for effect. It is clarified by the condition. Consider a moment that requires no elaboration. A man is told that he will die if he remains. He remains. No argument accompanies the decision. No explanation is offered that would make it more acceptable or more intelligible. The man stands, and the outcome follows. The question is not what he believes. It is what he does. This is what the work presents. Not the justification of war, nor its strategy, nor its outcome, but the manner in which men meet what cannot be avoided once it is present.

The term *bearing* names this more precisely than any other. To bear is not merely to endure. It is to carry oneself within a condition without losing proportion. It is to act, or to refrain, in a manner that remains aligned with what one has already established. It is to meet what is before one without excess, without collapse, and without withdrawal from what must be done. This is not stated within the work. It is shown.

The difference between feeling and conduct is maintained throughout. Men experience anger, grief, fear, and pride. These are not concealed. They are present, and they are expressed. But they do not determine the value of the man. What matters is how he carries these states into action. A man may feel anger. What follows from it is what is seen. A man may grieve. How he conducts himself within that grief is what is measured. Feeling is not removed, but it is placed under condition.

Achilles is central not because he is without fault, but because he reveals this pattern clearly. He withdraws, and others suffer. He returns, and the field changes. He exceeds, and the consequence of excess becomes visible. He is brought to a point at which recognition occurs, not through instruction, but through what has followed from what he has done. Nothing is concealed. Nothing is explained away. The movement is direct.

It is often said that this is a tragic work. If this is so, the tragedy lies not in the inevitability of death, but in the clarity with which conduct is exposed before it. A man is not hidden within circumstance. He is revealed by it. War does not create this condition. It removes what would otherwise obscure it.

The reader who approaches this work in search of explanation may find much to consider: the causes of conflict, the structure of the narrative, the interplay of forces beyond the human. These are present, and they may be examined. But if he begins there, he will miss what is most immediate. He will not see the man.

To approach this work as it was first received, the reader must attend to what is done before asking what it means. He must observe the sequence.

A man refuses.

Others suffer.

A man stands.

He falls.

A man returns.

The field alters.

Nothing in these sequences is hidden. They do not require interpretation to be understood. They require only that the reader remain with them long enough to see what follows from what is done.

This is why *The Iliad* is not about war in the ordinary sense. War provides the condition in which bearing is made visible. Without it, the same patterns might appear, but they would be less clear: delayed, mediated, or concealed by circumstances that permit ambiguity. Here, they are exposed.

The condition is particular. The pattern is not.

It is enough that it is seen here.

Chapter 6
Achilles: The Fracture and the Return

The movement of *The Iliad* is not carried by the war alone. It is carried by a man. Achilles stands at the center, not because he is the strongest, but because what occurs in him is made visible without concealment. He does not represent a principle. He reveals a sequence. It begins with injury. The injury is not physical. It is a wound to standing. A claim is made against him; something is taken; a limit is imposed. He does not accept it. He does not negotiate it. He withdraws. The withdrawal is immediate. It is complete in its effect, though not in its form. He remains present, but he does not act. He refuses to carry what he had carried before.

The consequence follows. The army suffers. No argument is attached to this. No explanation is given to make the sequence easier to accept. It is shown. A man removes himself, and others bear what he has set down.

This is the fracture. It is not the anger itself that produces it. Anger is present throughout the work; it does not, in itself, determine the course. The fracture occurs when anger passes into refusal, and refusal is carried without regard for what follows beyond the man who holds it.

The pattern is simple. A man places himself at the center of what must be borne. He withdraws from it. The burden shifts. It does not disappear. Time passes within the telling, but the position holds. Others act. They speak, advance, retreat, and fall. The field continues without him, but not without consequence. The absence is not neutral. It is felt in what fails to occur.

Attempts are made to restore him. He is offered what was taken. He is addressed with care. He is reminded of what stands beyond his injury. He does not return. The refusal remains. This is not presented as strength. It is not presented as weakness. It is presented as fact. He has chosen, and he continues in that choice.

The return does not come through persuasion. It comes through loss.

Patroclus enters the field in his place.

He takes up what Achilles has set down.

He acts, and he is killed.

The sequence is direct. A man refuses. Another bears. The consequence arrives where it must. There is no mediation between the action and its result. The return is immediate. Achilles does not deliberate. He does not reconsider his position in light of new arguments. He moves. He re-enters the field with a force that exceeds what was before. The restraint that was absent in his withdrawal is absent in his return. He does not resume his former place. He passes beyond it. This, too, is shown without explanation.

The man who withheld now does not withhold. The measure that was abandoned remains absent. What had been held in anger is released in action.

The field changes.

Men fall.

Opposition is met without pause. The sequence accelerates. What had been delayed now proceeds without interruption. This is not restoration. It is excess. *The Iliad* does not halt here. It does not conclude with the return, nor does it resolve itself in victory. It continues beyond the point at which the expected pattern might end.

Hector is killed.

The act itself is not isolated. It is followed. The body is not returned. It is taken, displayed, and subjected to treatment that exceeds what the moment requires. The action continues after its necessity has passed. The excess is made visible. No statement accompanies it. No judgment is given in words. It is shown in what is done beyond what must be done. The final movement is not another battle. It is a meeting. Priam comes to Achilles. He enters the place of the man who has killed his son. He speaks, not in challenge, but in recognition. He does not argue. He does not accuse. He places before Achilles what cannot be set aside. A father stands before the man who has taken his son. Nothing in this requires explanation. Achilles listens and receives him.

The sequence shifts. What has been carried in anger, in refusal, and in excess, is met by something that does not oppose it, but reveals it. The man who has acted without measure is brought into relation with what lies beyond his own position.

The body is returned.

The action is simple. No speech declares the meaning of what has occurred. No conclusion is drawn. The excess ceases.

This is the return. It is not a return to the beginning. It is not a restoration of what was lost. It is a re-establishment of proportion after its abandonment. Achilles does not become another man. He is not corrected in speech or instructed in principle. He acts differently. What had been carried without measure is set within it.

The sequence, taken as a whole, is clear.

Injury.

Withdrawal.

Consequence.

Loss.

Return.

Excess.

Recognition.

Restraint.

Nothing in this sequence is hidden. It is not arranged to persuade. It is presented. The reader may be inclined to divide it into parts: to separate anger from action, action from consequence, consequence from recognition. The poem does not divide it. It allows each movement to follow from the last.

This is why the text does not require interpretation to be understood. It shows what occurs when a man departs from what he bears, and what follows when he returns without measure. It shows what is required to bring that movement to rest. It does not state this. It allows it to be seen.

To approach this sequence properly, the reader must remain within it. He must not begin by asking whether Achilles is justified, whether his anger is warranted, or whether his actions are proportioned. These questions may arise. They are not first. What is first is what is done, and what follows. Seen in action, the sequence is simpler.

> A man refuses.
>
> Others suffer.
>
> A man returns.
>
> He exceeds.
>
> He is met.
>
> He ceases.

Nothing more is required for the sequence to be understood. From this, something becomes visible that does not depend upon the setting. The condition is particular. The pattern is not.

> A man is injured.
>
> He withdraws from what he bears.
>
> Others carry what he has set down.
>
> He returns without measure.
>
> The consequence extends beyond what is required.
>
> He is brought into relation with what lies beyond himself.
>
> He acts differently.

This is not confined to the battlefield, though the reader must first see it there.

Chapter 7
The Gods as Forces

The gods are present throughout *The Iliad*. They speak, act, oppose, and intervene. They appear beside men, move among them, and alter the course of events. They favor, restrain, deceive, and assist. Nothing in the work suggests that they are distant or removed. They are near.

From this, a conclusion is often drawn: that the work presents a world governed by divine personalities. This is not precise. The gods are not presented as characters in the same sense as the men. They are personalities in form, but forces in function. They do not develop, reconsider, or change in response to what occurs. They do not learn. They do not arrive at recognition. What they do remains consistent with what they are. They are better understood as forces. Each god acts in accordance with a particular order.

Ares enters the field without restraint. Where he appears, violence accelerates. Measure is lost. Action becomes immediate, unconsidered, and excessive. There is no sequence, only impact.

Athena acts otherwise. She does not remove conflict. She orders it. She directs action, restrains impulse, and aligns means with ends. Where she is present, movement becomes precise. What is done is done with awareness of what follows.

The distinction is not explained. It is shown. When these forces meet, the result is not a debate. It is an outcome. One prevails, not by argument, but by the nature of what it is. The poem does not question which is preferable. It shows what follows from each.

The same pattern appears across the field. A man advances under one influence; another acts under a different one. The gods do not replace human action. They reveal its direction. A man who moves without measure does not become so because a god has entered him. The presence of the god makes visible the form his action has taken. What might otherwise appear mixed or uncertain is clarified by association. This is why the gods are near. They do not obscure the human field. They sharpen it.

It is possible to read these appearances as external interventions: as moments in which events are altered by powers beyond the human. This reading is not without basis. The work presents the gods as active, and their actions have effect. But this is not the only way in which they operate. They also make visible what would otherwise remain less distinct. A man hesitates. He is steadied. A man rushes forward. He is not checked. A decision is made, and the consequence aligns with the force under which it was taken. The presence of the god marks the movement. The reader does not need to decide whether the god caused the action or accompanied it. He needs only to observe the alignment.

This is why the gods do not require interpretation to be understood. They do not conceal their nature. They do not present themselves in forms that must be decoded. They act, and what follows corresponds. Where there is disorder, excess, and immediate violence, one force is present. Where there is measure, restraint, and directed action, another is at work. The story does not ask the reader to believe in these figures. It asks him to see what is shown when they appear.

The relation between the human and the divine is therefore not one of replacement. The gods do not remove responsibility from men. They do not act in place of them. The field remains human. Men speak, choose, and act. They bear the consequence. The gods mark the form of those actions. They make clear what might otherwise remain obscured by complexity or delay. This can be seen without argument. A man enters the field without restraint. The action accelerates; consequence follows immediately. Another holds, considers, and directs. The movement is different; the result aligns.

The Iliad does not assign these patterns to abstract categories. It places them before the reader as forces that can be recognized in what is done. This is why the gods do not stand apart from the work. They are not additions to it. They are part of the way in which it presents its field. Without them, the same actions might occur, but their form would be less distinct. The presence of the gods sharpens the line between what is ordered and what is not. They bring the pattern forward.

The modern reader may be inclined to resolve this into explanation: to determine whether the gods are symbolic, psychological, or theological in nature. Each of these approaches seeks to place the gods within a framework that can be accounted for. The poem does not require this. It presents them in action.

To begin with explanation is to step away from what is shown. To remain with what is shown is sufficient.

A force enters.

Action follows.

A different force is present.

The movement changes.

Nothing more is required for the distinction to be seen. From this, a clarity emerges that does not depend upon belief. The reader need not decide what the gods are in order to see what occurs when they appear. He need only attend to the pattern that accompanies them.

Where action loses measure, something is present. Where action holds its line, something else is at work. The names given to these presences are not the point. What matters is what follows from them. The reader is not instructed in this. Instead it is placed before him. If he remains with it, the distinction becomes clear. If he departs into explanation too soon, it becomes obscured.

The gods do not replace what men do. They reveal it.

What is revealed does not require belief. It requires only that it be seen.

Chapter 8
Honor, Grief, and
the Treatment of the Dead

The Iliad does not end with the fall of a man. It continues in what follows. When a man is killed, the action does not conclude with the blow. What is done with the body that remains is part of the same field. It reveals whether proportion has been maintained or abandoned, whether what has been taken in conflict is held within order or carried beyond it. This is not presented as a custom. It is shown as conduct.

Patroclus is killed.

The fact is immediate. It does not require amplification. The response follows at once, not in explanation, but in action. The body is recovered. It is guarded. It is prepared. Nothing in this sequence is excessive. What is done corresponds to what has occurred. The man is not treated as an object to be removed, nor as a symbol to be displayed. He is returned to those to whom he belongs, and he is given what is required.

Grief is present.

It is not concealed. It is not moderated for appearance. It appears as it does, and it is carried forward into what must be done. The preparation of the body proceeds within it. The rites are performed within it. The grief does not interrupt the sequence; it accompanies it.

This is the first pattern. Grief does not replace conduct. It enters it. The treatment of Hector presents another.

He is killed in the field.

The act is not isolated. It is followed. The body is taken. It is not returned. It is subjected to treatment that extends beyond what the moment requires. The action does not stop where necessity ends. It continues. This continuation is not explained. It is shown.

The difference between the two sequences is not stated. It is visible. A body is recovered, prepared, and returned within measure. Another is taken, held, and subjected to excess. In both cases, grief is present. In both cases, loss is real. What differs is the manner in which these are carried into action. In one, proportion holds. In the other, it does not. The reader may be inclined to separate these as different kinds of acts: one proper, the other improper. The work does not divide them in this way. It presents both within the same field. The same man is present in both.

Achilles grieves.

He acts.

He exceeds.

No transition explains the movement. No speech marks the point at which grief passes into excess. The sequence is continuous.

This is the second pattern. A man may remain aligned with what he bears. He may also pass beyond it. The return from excess is not achieved through instruction. It does not come from correction in speech or the application of principle. It comes from encounter.

Priam comes to Achilles.

He does not enter as an adversary. He does not demand. He does not argue. He presents what cannot be set aside: a father before the man who has taken his son. The meeting alters the field. No explanation accompanies it. No reasoning is offered that would account for the change. The action that follows is simple.

The body is returned.

This is not a resolution in the sense of conclusion. The war does not end. The loss is not undone. What has occurred remains. What changes is the manner in which it is carried. The excess ceases.

The distinction made here is exact. It is not between grief and its absence. It is between grief carried within proportion and grief carried beyond it. The poem does not remove grief. It does not ask that it be suppressed or transformed into something else. It allows it to appear in its full force. What it shows is how that force is borne. This is why the treatment of the dead occupies so much of the work. It is not incidental. It is not a matter of custom alone. It is the point at which conduct is revealed without mediation.

A man has acted.

Another has fallen.

What remains is the body. What is done with it cannot be deferred, and it cannot be concealed. It is visible, immediate, and final. In this moment, there is no distance between action and consequence. The reader does not need to be instructed in what is proper. He sees it. A body is prepared with care, returned, and honored. Another is held beyond necessity, subjected to continued action that serves no further requirement. Nothing in these sequences requires explanation. They present themselves.

From this, something becomes clear. Conflict does not end when a man falls. It continues in how what remains is treated. If proportion is maintained, the field is brought back within order. If it is not, the disorder extends. This is not a moral claim. It is a sequence. The text does not state this. It allows it to be seen.

Grief is present in both cases. Loss is real in both. What differs is the line that is held or abandoned in response. The reader may be inclined to ask why one sequence is carried within measure and the other is not. On this, *The Iliad* is silent. It shows what follows in each case.

To approach this properly, the reader must remain with the action. He must not move at once to judgment or explanation. He must attend to what is done, and to what follows from it.

A man grieves.

He prepares.

A man grieves.

He exceeds.

A man is met.

He returns.

The condition is particular. The pattern is not.

Chapter 9
How to Die Properly

The phrase may appear severe. It is easily misunderstood. To speak of dying "properly" is not to prescribe an outcome, nor to suggest that death itself can be arranged in a manner that satisfies intention. Death, in this work, is not governed. It arrives where it will. It does not wait upon readiness, nor does it adjust itself to preference.

The Iliad does not teach how to avoid death. It shows how a man bears himself when it cannot be avoided. In the poem, death is not distant. It is present throughout. It does not appear as an interruption, but as a condition within which all action occurs. Men advance knowing what may follow. They speak under that condition. They choose within it. Nothing in this requires emphasis. The reader does not need to be told what is at stake. When a man stands before death, the question is not whether he will survive. It is how he will stand. This is shown without instruction.

A man is warned.

He advances.

A man is pressed.

He holds.

A man is struck.

He falls.

In each case, what matters is not the fact of death, but the manner in which it is met. The account does not isolate a single example and raise it above the others. It presents many.

A man speaks before he advances. He names what stands before him. He does not conceal it. He does not deny it. He places it within his own action and proceeds.

Another hesitates. He considers. He measures. He enters when he must.

Another turns away. He withdraws from what he had approached.

The outcomes differ. The pattern remains. To die properly is not to choose death. It is to remain aligned with oneself when death is present. This alignment does not require stillness. It does not exclude action. It is not a matter of posture in the narrow sense. It is a matter of proportion. A man may advance with force. He may hold position. He may retreat. Each of these may be done within proportion, or beyond it.

The work does not favor one form over another. It shows what follows from each. This is why the story does not elevate death itself. It does not present it as noble, nor as tragic in the abstract. It does not surround it with language that would separate it from the conditions in which it occurs. It places it within sequence.

A man acts.

The consequence follows.

Nothing more is required. The reader may be inclined to seek meaning in the fact of death: to ask what it signifies, what it represents, or what it reveals about the world in which it occurs. The poem does not proceed in this way. It does not extract death from action. It shows death as the end of a sequence that begins with conduct.

This is where the phrase takes its meaning. To die properly is to carry oneself within that sequence without departure. It is to act without excess, without collapse, and without withdrawal from what must be borne. It is to meet what stands before one without seeking to escape it through explanation or denial. This is not stated. It is shown.

Hector stands before Achilles. He is aware of what follows. He does not mistake the condition in which he stands.

He turns away.

He runs.

He is pursued.

He stops.

He turns.

He stands.

The outcome is not in question. The manner is. Nothing in the work instructs the reader to admire this. Nothing directs him to condemn it. It is presented. The recognition, if it occurs, is his.

The same clarity appears elsewhere. A man falls without warning. Another calls out. Another does not. Each action is complete in itself. Each carries forward into consequence. No arrangement is made to distinguish one from the other beyond what is done.

This is the field. The work does not provide a rule. It provides a series of moments in which the same condition is met in different ways. From these, the sequence becomes visible. A man who remains aligned with what he bears does not depart from himself when death is present. A man who has already departed cannot recover alignment in that moment.

Nothing is added at the end. What was present before remains present at the close. There is no consolation. It does not offer a resolution that would soften what has occurred. It does not promise that what is lost is restored elsewhere, nor does it place death within a larger assurance. It leaves the sequence as it stands.

A man stands.

He knows.

He acts.

Consequence follows.

The manner remains. To approach this properly, the reader must resist the impulse to look beyond the moment. He must remain within it. From this, something becomes clear that does not depend upon the field. Where death is present, the question is not how it may be avoided, but how a man remains within himself when it arrives.

Nothing else is required.

Part III:
The Odyssey: How a Man Lives

Chapter 10
The Man of Many Turns

The work known as *The Odyssey* does not begin where the previous one ends. It does not carry forward the same field. The war is past. The conditions are altered. What remains is not the pressure of conflict, but the absence of it, and the uncertainty that follows. A man is no longer placed before what must be met at once. He is placed within what must be navigated.

Odysseus is not defined by a single movement. He does not stand in one place and hold. He does not withdraw and return in the same manner. He moves. The work names him in this way: a man of many turns.[1] This is not a description of inconsistency. It is a description of continuity under changing conditions.

The field in which he acts does not remain stable. The sea shifts. The shore is uncertain. The men who accompany him are not constant in their conduct. Those who receive him do not do so in the same way. Nothing in his path allows him to proceed in a single, fixed manner from beginning to end. What would hold in one place fails in another. What is required changes.

In such a field, constancy does not appear as repetition. It appears as alignment. A man may speak differently, act differently, and take on different forms, yet remain continuous with himself. The measure is not whether his actions are the same, but whether they remain within the line he has established.

This is the first distinction.

---

[1] The Greek term is *polytropos* (πολύτροπος), often rendered as "resourceful," "wily," or "of many ways." Such translations tend to reduce the term to a trait. The original carries a broader sense of movement and adaptability across changing conditions.

Odysseus speaks when it is required. He withholds when it is not. He names himself, and he conceals his name. He advances, and he delays. He accepts what is given, and he refuses what would bind him beyond his purpose. These are not contradictions. They are adjustments.

The poem does not present a man who is fixed. It presents a man who does not lose himself as conditions change. This is not achieved by holding to a single form of action. It is achieved by remaining within a line that can be carried through different forms.

The reader may be inclined to resolve these into a single trait: cleverness, cunning, or strategy. These terms are not incorrect, but they are not sufficient. They describe what is done. They do not describe how it is held.

The difference becomes clear when that line is broken. At times, Odysseus exceeds. He speaks when silence would have held. He reveals what could have remained concealed. He acts beyond what the moment requires. The consequence follows. It does not arrive as correction in speech. It arrives as extension of what has been set in motion. Time is lengthened. Distance increases. What might have been contained continues.

These moments are not exceptions. They are part of the same movement.

A man adjusts.

A man exceeds.

The consequence follows.

He returns to measure.

Nothing in this requires explanation. The work proceeds through a series of encounters.

A place is reached. It is not known.

A decision is made. A course is taken.

The result appears. The man continues.

Each encounter differs in form. The movement remains. In one place, a man is received and offered what would remove him from his path. He considers. He refuses. In another, he is tested through deception. He responds with deception. In another, he is brought to the edge of dissolution. He holds. The reader does not need to unify these through interpretation. He sees what is done.

This is the second distinction. Where the earlier work shows a man under a fixed condition, this one shows a man within shifting ones.

The question is no longer: How does a man stand when he cannot move? It becomes: How does a man remain himself when he must move constantly? The answer is not stated. It is shown. The reader may be inclined to extract a rule: to determine what the man should do in each case, or what principle governs his action. *The Odyssey* does not proceed in this way. It presents situations. It shows responses. It allows consequence to follow. From these, something becomes visible. Not a rule, but a line.

A man who is carried by circumstance is altered by it. A man who carries himself through circumstance remains aligned. The difference is not in what he encounters. It is in how he meets it.

There is no reward for a single form of action. Force alone does not suffice. Nor does caution. Nor does deception. Nor does openness. Each is used. Each has its place. What matters is whether the man who uses them remains within measure.

The term *many turns* names this precisely. It does not indicate wandering. It indicates movement that does not depart from itself.

To approach this properly, the reader must remain with the movement. He must not fix upon a single moment and take it as representative of the whole. He must not isolate one action and raise it above the others. He must observe the sequence across change.

A man speaks.

He withholds.

He advances.

He waits.

He reveals.

He conceals.

The forms change. The line remains.

It is enough that it is seen.

Chapter 11
Storms and Shipwrecks

The sea does not hold its shape. It does not remain where it is placed, nor does it proceed in a line that can be followed. It rises, falls, breaks, and reforms without regard for what stands upon it. It does not answer to intention. It does not adjust itself to expectation. In *The Odyssey*, this condition is not introduced as an obstacle to be overcome. It is given as the field.

A man sets out with purpose. He intends to go from one place to another. He prepares, gathers what is required, and proceeds. The beginning is clear. What follows is not. The course does not hold. The direction is altered. The distance extends. The man is carried where he did not intend to go. What he had set before himself recedes. This is not an interruption. It is the condition.

The reader may be inclined to ask why this occurs. No answer is offered. There is no presentation of a system by which the sea may be understood or predicted. It does not offer a method by which uncertainty may be reduced. It shows a man within uncertainty.

Odysseus is not in control of the field. This is made clear at once. He acts, and the result does not follow his intention. He prepares, and what he has prepared is undone. He proceeds, and the course is altered. Nothing in this requires emphasis. The man does not command the condition. From this, a question arises.

Not: How does he control what is before him?

But: How does he act when he cannot?

The work answers in sequence. A storm comes. The man does not argue with it. He does not attempt to master it through assertion or denial. He meets it. He holds what can be held. He releases what must be released. He acts within the moment as it presents itself. The outcome is not secured. The action is.

This is the first pattern. When control is absent, collapse is not required.

The differentiation between the two is exact. A man may lose control of the field. He need not lose himself within it.

The Odyssey does not present this as a principle. It shows it. A ship is driven off course. The men respond. They attempt to hold their line. The line breaks. The vessel is lost. The man remains.

The reader may be inclined to see this as endurance. It is not endurance alone. It is the maintenance of alignment under conditions that do not permit control.

There is no illusion here. The work does not suggest that the man will succeed because he acts well. It does not reward proportion with outcome. It does not promise that the one who holds will be carried safely through. The field does not answer to conduct in this way.

What the work shows is different. A man who collapses under such a condition is lost before the outcome arrives. A man who holds remains present to what follows. The difference is not in the result. It is in the manner.

This becomes clearer as the sequence continues. A man is separated from what he has gathered. He loses those who accompanied him. He is left alone. What had been shared is no longer present. What had been carried together is now borne by one. The condition has altered. The man remains.

No explanation is given that would account for why one survives and another does not. No principle is offered that would guarantee preservation. There is no attempt to make the outcome intelligible in this way. It shows what is done when the outcome cannot be secured.

A man is thrown into the water. He does not stand. He does not command. He is carried. Yet even here, action remains. He chooses when to hold, when to release, when to move, when to remain still. The field is not his to govern. The moment is.

This is the second pattern. When the field cannot be governed, the moment still can.

The reader does not need to reconcile this with expectation. He sees it. A man is stripped of control. He does not collapse. A man is driven off course. He continues. A man is reduced to what he can carry. He carries it.

Nothing in these sequences is elevated. They are presented without emphasis. The sea does not change. The man does not command it. He remains within himself as it moves.

This is why there is no offer of a method. It does not provide instruction on how to navigate the sea. It does not teach the reader how to avoid what cannot be avoided. It shows how a man acts when he is already within it.

The reader may be inclined to extract a lesson: to determine what should be done, or what principle governs the action. *The Odyssey* does not proceed in this way. It presents a series of moments. From these, something becomes visible. Not control. Not mastery. Alignment.

A man who seeks to impose himself upon the field is broken by it. A man who yields entirely is carried without direction. A man who remains within himself acts where he can, and does not depart where he cannot.

The term *shipwreck* does not name failure alone. It names a condition in which what has been prepared is no longer sufficient, and what remains must be carried forward without it. The poem does not treat this as an end. It continues from it.

To approach this properly, the reader must remain within the condition. He must not move at once to outcome. He must not ask how the man will reach his destination, nor how long the journey will take. These questions may arise. They are not first. What is first is what is done when the course is lost.

A man is driven off line.

He does not abandon himself.

A man is cast into the water.

He acts within the moment.

The field is unstable. The man need not be.

Chapter 12
The Sirens, Circe, and
the Nature of Temptation

The work proceeds through encounters that do not present themselves as obstacles alone. They offer, attract, and invite. What stands before the man is not always force to be met or danger to be resisted. It is often something that draws him forward, not by compulsion, but by promise. This is the condition of temptation. It does not announce itself as threat. It appears as something to be taken up, something that offers advantage, knowledge, relief, or pleasure. The danger does not lie in what is presented, but in how it is received. *The Odyssey* does not define temptation. It shows what occurs when a man meets it.

The Sirens do not pursue. They remain where they are. They call. The call does not command; it invites. It promises something that cannot be obtained otherwise. It offers knowledge, or the appearance of it. It suggests that something essential will be gained by drawing nearer. Nothing in this requires elaboration. A man hears. He desires to hear more. He moves toward what calls him. The consequence is not delayed. Those who follow the call do not return.

Odysseus does not avoid the Sirens. He does not refuse to hear them. He does not deny the presence of what they offer. He prepares. He has himself bound. He places others under instruction. He arranges the encounter before entering it. When the moment comes:

He hears.

He is drawn.

He struggles.

He calls to be released.

He is not released.

The sequence is complete. Nothing in this requires interpretation. A man enters an encounter that cannot be met without preparation. He does not trust himself within it. He establishes a limit in advance. When the moment exceeds what he can carry, the limit holds. This is the first form. Temptation is not removed; it is contained.

The work presents another. Circe does not call from a distance; she receives. Men enter. They are offered what appears to be sustenance. They accept. They are altered. The change is not gradual; it is immediate. Those who have entered without measure are no longer what they were. The difference between the two encounters is not in their nature, but in the manner in which they are met. In one, the man prepares; in the other, the men do not. The consequence follows.

Odysseus approaches Circe differently. He does not enter unguarded. He is equipped before he arrives. He does not refuse the encounter, but he does not receive it without measure. He acts within it, but he is not altered by it. The sequence holds. Nothing in this requires explanation. A man enters without preparation; he is changed. A man enters with preparation; he is not. This is the second form. Temptation is not always resisted; it is met.

The reader may be inclined to divide these into moral distinctions: to separate what is permitted from what is forbidden, to determine what should be refused and what may be accepted. The poem does not proceed in this way. It does not provide a rule. It presents a series of encounters in which the same condition is met under different forms. From these, something becomes visible. A man who receives without measure is taken by what he receives. A man who remains within measure may take without being taken. The difference is not in what is offered. It is in how it is held.

This holds across the work. A place is reached. It offers rest. A man remains beyond what is required. The movement is delayed. The path extends. Another place offers the same. A man receives what is needed and continues. The outcome differs. The pattern holds. Temptation is not presented as exceptional. It is continuous. At each point, something is offered that may alter the course. The form changes; the condition remains. The man must meet it.

To meet it properly, he must remain aligned with what he has set before himself. He must not abandon his line for what appears in the moment, however compelling it may be. He must not receive without limit, nor refuse without consideration. This is not stated. It is shown. Nothing more is required.

The reader is not asked to condemn what is offered. He is asked to see what follows from how it is received. From this, something becomes clear. Temptation does not act upon a man independently of his own conduct. It is completed in how he meets it.

> A man hears; he prepares.
> A man enters; he is changed.
> A man enters again; he remains.

Temptation is not completed in what appears. It is completed in how it is met.

Chapter 13
Polyphemus: Strength Without Order

The work presents forms of power that do not require naming in order to be recognized. They appear in action, and their nature is made visible by what follows from them. Among these, one stands apart for its clarity.

Polyphemus does not belong to the world of measured exchange. He lives outside it. He does not assemble with others, does not bind himself to agreement, and does not receive according to any order that would permit a stranger to enter without risk. What he has is sufficient to him. What stands before him is taken as it appears. Nothing in this requires explanation. A man enters his dwelling. He is not received. He is held. Food is not offered. It is taken. The distinction between host and guest does not exist. The structure that would govern such an encounter is absent. This is the first indication. Where there is no order, strength is not directed. It acts upon what is before it.

The reader may be inclined to see this as savagery, or to separate it from the rest of the work as something extreme. The telling does not make this separation. It presents a condition in which force is present without proportion. Polyphemus does not conceal what he is. He does not deceive. He does not persuade. He does not arrange. He acts. What he does follows directly from what he is.

Odysseus enters this condition without its protections. He comes as he would elsewhere, expecting the forms that permit an encounter to proceed without immediate conflict. He finds none. The expectation does not hold. The situation alters at once. There is no appeal to be made. Speech does not bind.

Custom does not restrain. Nothing stands between the man and what is before him except what he can bring to bear within the moment. This is the field.

Force alone does not answer it. To meet unbounded force with force is to enter the same condition without altering it. The outcome is not in question. What is required is not an increase of strength, but a change in relation. Odysseus does not attempt to overcome Polyphemus directly. He does not match what cannot be matched. He alters the condition. He speaks. He names himself in a manner that removes what would otherwise fix him. He gives a name that cannot be held. The act is simple. Its effect is not. When the moment comes and force seeks to extend itself beyond what is before it, the name does not carry. The call for response does not arrive where it would be received. Nothing in this requires elaboration. A man changes how he is known. The consequence follows.

This is the first movement. When strength is without order, it can be redirected by altering the field in which it acts.

The second movement follows. Polyphemus is not persuaded. He is not corrected. He is not brought into measure. He remains what he is. Odysseus does not attempt to change him. He acts within what is given. He blinds him. The act is exact. It does not remove strength. It removes sight. What was acting without limit can no longer act with direction. The consequence is immediate. Force remains. It no longer governs. Nothing in this is presented as a triumph. It is an adjustment. A condition is met. The response aligns with what is required to pass through it.

The reader may be inclined to assign meaning to the act, to determine what it represents, or what principle it illustrates. The story does not proceed in this way. It presents a sequence. A man is held within a condition without order. He alters how he is known. He removes the capacity of the force before him to act with direction. He departs. Nothing more is required.

The movement does not end there. As the man departs, he speaks. He names himself. The name that had been withheld is now given. The action that had been contained extends beyond what is required for departure. What had been held within measure passes beyond it. The consequence follows. The condition is extended. What might have ended does not end. This is not separated from what precedes it. It is part of the same sequence.

A man adjusts.

A man escapes.

A man exceeds.

The consequence extends.

The reader is not instructed to condemn this, nor is excuse provided. Instead he is shown what follows. What is required to meet the condition is one thing. What is done beyond that requirement is another. The difference is not stated. It is visible in the sequence.

From this, something becomes clear. Strength without order cannot be engaged directly. It must be met by altering the relation in which it acts. But the man who does so is not exempt from measure. If he departs from it, the consequence follows beyond the moment.

Strength without order cannot be met directly. It must be met by altering the relation in which it acts.

The man who does so is not exempt from measure.

Chapter 14
The House Restored

The movement of *The Odyssey* does not end at the shore. Return is not arrival. A man reaches his house, and the condition does not resolve. It is revealed.

The house has not remained as it was. It has been entered without measure. Those who occupy it do not belong to it; they take what is not theirs, remain beyond their place, speak without restraint, and act without proportion. The structure that holds a house together has been set aside. What remains is not order, but occupation. Nothing in this requires explanation. A place that receives without limit cannot hold.

This is not presented as misfortune. It is presented as condition. The disorder is not hidden, nor is it partial. It extends through the house, shaping those within it and those who serve it. What had been structured has become unbounded. The work does not separate this from what preceded it. It is the same pattern. Where measure is abandoned, disorder extends.

Odysseus does not enter the house as himself. He does not announce his return or claim what is his at once. He enters concealed, observes, and tests. The sequence is deliberate. He does not act upon appearance; he determines what is present.

This is the first movement. A man returns to what is his, and does not assume it remains so.

Within the house, conduct is revealed. Some recognize; some do not. Some remain aligned; others have departed from what they once held. The distinctions are not stated. They appear in action. A man speaks, another responds; a servant acts, another refuses. Each movement places the man within the field that now exists. Nothing is explained. The reader sees what holds and what does not.

The Odyssey does not present reform. It does not offer correction in speech, nor does it attempt to restore order through persuasion. The condition has passed beyond that point. What is required is not adjustment, but re-establishment.

The action that follows is direct. The house is closed. Those within it are held in place. What has been taken without measure is met with force. What has exceeded its bounds is brought to an end. The sequence proceeds without interruption. This is not presented as excess. It is proportioned to the condition.

The reader may be inclined to see this as revenge but this is not the governing structure. Revenge seeks satisfaction; this action restores propriety. The distinction is exact. Revenge continues beyond what is required; restoration ends when order is re-established.

The reader may ask whether another path was possible, whether the outcome could have been achieved through other means, whether the action is proportioned to the offense. These questions may arise. They are not first. What is first is the condition, and what follows from it. Where a structure has been entered without limit, it cannot be restored by appeal to those who have abandoned limit. Where measure is no longer recognized, it cannot be reintroduced through agreement. The work does not state this. It shows what follows. Order is not maintained by intention alone; it is held through proportion. When proportion is abandoned, order does not remain in place. To restore it requires action that corresponds to the condition.

The movement concludes when the house is again aligned with what it must be. Those who belong remain. Those who do not are removed. The condition settles. Nothing in this requires justification. There is no argument for the necessity of what is done, nor is it defended. A sequence is presented.

A house is without order.

A man returns.

He observes.

He acts.

The order is restored.

The house stands.

The condition holds.

The man remains.

That is enough.

Chapter 15
Penelope: Order Held in Absence

The house does not stand by walls alone. It holds by what is maintained within it.

Penelope is present throughout the disorder. She does not depart. She does not withdraw from the place that has been entered without measure. She remains within it. Nothing in this requires emphasis. A woman stands within a house that no longer holds. She sees what is before her. She is not untouched by it, nor is she removed from it. She lives within it. She does not yield.

The condition around her does not change. Those who occupy the house continue as they have. They take what is not theirs. They speak without restraint. They press for conclusion. They seek to bring what is held to an end. She delays. The delay is not passive. It is not the absence of action. It is action held within measure.

She establishes a condition within the condition. What is demanded is not given at once. What is required is not refused outright. She does not confront directly, and she does not concede. She creates time. The form is simple. She sets a task. She undertakes it. She continues it. By day, it advances. By night, it is undone. The sequence repeats. Nothing in this requires explanation. What is presented as movement is not allowed to conclude. What appears to approach an end is returned to its beginning. The pressure remains. The demand does not resolve. Time is held.

This is not deception in the sense of concealment alone. It is proportion under pressure. The reader may be inclined to separate this from the movement of the work, to see it as delay without direction or resistance without force. No such separation is made. A form of conduct is put forth that does not advance, but does not collapse. A line is held without movement.

To hold is not to remain still. It is to remain aligned within a condition that presses toward change. Penelope does not abandon what must be borne. She does not accept what would dissolve the structure she maintains. She does not act beyond what is required to hold it. The pressure does not cease. The line remains — she does not yield what she has been holding.

A man moves.

A woman holds.

The condition remains.

The line remains.

The sequence is not elevated. It is not presented as virtue, nor does it surround it with praise. It shows what follows from it. The house does not collapse. The demand does not conclude. The condition is extended. This is not resolution. It is preservation.

The sequence continues until the moment of return. When Odysseus enters the house, she does not yield at once. She does not accept what appears before her without measure. She tests. What has been held cannot be surrendered without recognition. What has been preserved must be confirmed.

The test is exact. A sign is given that cannot be mistaken. What is known to her is placed before him. What cannot be altered is used to determine what stands before her. He responds. The recognition is complete. Nothing in this requires elaboration. What has been held is now aligned with what has returned.

To hold is not to accept without measure. It is to receive when alignment is present. The movement of the house is therefore not completed by force alone. It is completed by recognition. The house stands — not because it was untouched, but because it was held. Odysseus restores what has been entered without limit. Penelope confirms what is restored. The two movements meet.

A woman holds.
The condition remains.
The man returns.
The house stands.
What is restored is recognized.
The line holds.
That is enough.

Chapter 16
How to Live Properly

The phrase may invite a misunderstanding. To speak of living "properly" is not to prescribe a form of life, nor to establish a rule by which conduct is measured in advance. Life, as presented in *The Odyssey*, does not proceed under fixed conditions. It does not hold still long enough to be ordered from the outside. It moves, alters, and presents itself in forms that cannot be anticipated in full. The work does not teach how to arrange life. It shows how a man carries himself within it.

If the earlier work places a man within a condition he cannot avoid, this one places him within conditions that do not remain. The question is no longer how to stand when one cannot move, but how to remain aligned when one must move continually. This is not answered in statement. It is shown in sequence.

A man sets out with a purpose, and does not proceed in a straight line. He is diverted, delayed, received, tested, aided, and opposed. What appears before him changes, and what is required changes with it. He speaks differently in one place than in another. He acts openly in one moment and withholds in the next. He advances when the moment allows it and waits when it does not. Nothing in this is fixed. What holds is not the form of his action, but the line within it.

This is why the work does not present a single model to be followed. Force alone does not suffice. Caution alone does not suffice. Openness alone does not suffice. Each appears. Each is used. Each proves insufficient when carried beyond its place. The work does not resolve this into a principle. It presents a man who does not lose himself as he moves through these changes.

Odysseus speaks when it is required and withholds when it is not. He reveals himself and conceals himself. He accepts what is given and refuses what would bind him beyond his purpose. These are not contradictions. They are adjustments. The measure is not whether his actions remain the same, but whether they remain aligned with what he has set before himself. When that alignment is held, movement does not dissolve him. When it is abandoned, the consequence follows.

The work does not conceal these moments. He speaks when silence would have held. He reveals what could have remained concealed. He extends himself beyond what the moment requires. The effect is not correction but extension. What might have been contained continues. Time lengthens. Distance increases. The sequence is clear.

A man adjusts.

A man exceeds.

He returns to measure.

Nothing more is required. The reader may be inclined to seek a rule within these sequences, to determine what should be done in each case or what principle governs the action. The work does not proceed in this way. It does not provide instruction that can be applied apart from the condition in which it appears. It presents a field in which a man must act without the assurance that what holds in one moment will hold in the next.

From this, something becomes visible. A man who is carried by circumstance is altered by it. A man who carries himself through circumstance remains aligned. The difference is not in what he encounters. It is in how he meets it. This is the meaning of living properly as the work presents it: not adherence to a fixed form, but continuity within change; not the repetition of a single action, but the preservation of a line across many actions; not control of the field, but alignment within it.

The work does not elevate this. It does not present it as an achievement to be admired, nor does it separate it from failure.

It shows it in motion, alongside moments in which it is lost and regained.

A man holds.

A man departs.

A man returns.

Nothing in this requires explanation. The reader may be inclined to judge the man by individual actions, to isolate a moment and take it as representative of the whole. The work does not support this. It presents a sequence that must be seen across its movement.

A man speaks.

He withholds.

He advances.

He waits.

He reveals.

He conceals.

The forms change. The line remains.

The man returns — not as he began, and not as dissolved.

What has been encountered has not been avoided. What has been required has been met. What has been exceeded has been brought back within measure.

The line holds.

That is enough.

Part IV:
The Transmission of the Man

Chapter 17
Telemachus: Readiness Before Guidance

The movement of The Odyssey does not begin with the man who returns. It begins with the one who has not yet begun.

Telemachus is present within the house before it is restored. He stands within the condition that has formed around him. He sees what is before him, but he does not yet act within it. He is not prevented. He is not restrained by force. He remains where he is. Nothing in this requires explanation. A man stands within a condition that does not hold. He sees what does not align. He does not move.

The reader may be inclined to see this as weakness, or as failure of character. The work does not present it in this way. It presents a condition in which readiness has not yet formed. Readiness is not given. It does not arise from instruction alone. It does not come from the presence of another who acts in place of the man. It appears when what is seen can no longer be carried without response. This is not stated. It is shown.

Telemachus lives within disorder. The house is occupied. Those within it speak without measure. They take what is not theirs. They remain without limit. The structure that should govern the house is absent. He is not unaware of this. He sees it. He hears it. He moves within it. He does not act. The condition holds.

The change does not come from correction. No one instructs him in what must be done. No argument is presented that compels him forward. No example is placed before him that he is asked to imitate. The movement begins elsewhere. He reaches a point at which what he sees is no longer sufficient to carry without response.

A man sees and does not act.

A man sees and cannot remain.

The difference is not in what is seen. It is in what is borne.

At this point, guidance appears. Athena enters, not in her own form, but in a form that can be received. She does not announce herself as what she is. She does not present authority in a manner that would compel obedience. She speaks within the condition that is already present. She does not act in his place. She does not remove the disorder. She directs his attention.

The sequence is exact. She asks, and he responds. She points, and he sees. She urges, and he moves. Nothing in this requires elaboration.

Guidance does not produce readiness. It follows it. Where readiness is absent, guidance does not take hold. It may be heard, but it does not move the man. Where readiness is present, guidance aligns with what has already begun. It does not impose direction. It confirms it.

Telemachus begins to act. He speaks within the house. He calls those within it to account. He does not yet restore order. He does not yet alter the condition. He moves. This is sufficient. The work does not present this as transformation. It does not suggest that the man has become something else. It shows that he has begun to act within what he already is.

He departs. He leaves the house that has formed him and enters a field that is not his own. He speaks with others. He hears what is said. He sees what has been done before him. This is not instruction. It is exposure.

A man moves.

He listens.

He sees.

He returns.

What has changed is not the condition alone. The man has altered his relation to it. He no longer remains within it without response. He moves within it. He acts within it. He prepares for what must follow.

This is readiness. It is not knowledge. It is not certainty. It is not the possession of a plan that guarantees outcome. It is the point at which a man can no longer remain as he has been.

The work does not extend this into a doctrine of instruction. It does not present a method by which one man may shape another. It shows a sequence in which a man becomes able to receive what would otherwise pass without effect. From this, something becomes clear. A man cannot be formed from the outside. He may be directed, corrected, or instructed, but none of these produce readiness. They may accompany it. They may align with it. They do not create it.

The reader may be inclined to seek a rule here, to determine when guidance should be given or how it should be applied. The work does not proceed in this way. It shows what occurs when readiness appears, and how guidance meets it.

The man who has not yet begun stands within the condition. He sees. He does not move. Guidance appears. The man who is ready cannot remain. He acts.

The house remains disordered. The men within it continue as they have. Nothing is yet restored. What has changed is the posture of the man.

This is sufficient.

Chapter 18
Athena and Mentor

Guidance does not begin with instruction. It begins with recognition.

Athena does not appear as authority. She does not present herself in a form that would compel obedience. She does not stand above the man and declare what must be done. She comes first in a form that can be received, and later under the name and form of Mentor. This is not concealment for its own sake. It is proportion.

Telemachus is not ready to receive command. He is ready to receive alignment. What appears before him must meet him where he stands, not where he is not yet able to stand. Guidance that exceeds readiness does not take hold. It is heard, but it does not move the man.

Authority does not produce movement. Recognition does.

The sequence is exact. A presence enters that does not impose. It speaks within the condition already present. It does not replace what the man sees. It directs his attention to it. It does not act in his place. It reveals where action is already required. Nothing in this requires elaboration.

She asks, and he answers. She points, and he sees. She urges, and he moves. This is guidance. It does not supply what is absent. It aligns with what has begun.

The reader may be inclined to interpret this as instruction, to see in it a transfer of knowledge or a shaping of thought. The work does not proceed in this way. What is given is not information that the man did not possess. It is orientation within what he already sees. The difference is not in knowledge. It is in position.

Telemachus has seen the disorder. He has lived within it. He has heard what is said and observed what is done. What he lacks is not awareness, but readiness to act within it. Athena does not give him this readiness. She meets it.

A man sees and does not act. A man sees and cannot remain. The difference is not in what is seen. It is in what is borne.

Guidance does not create readiness. It follows it.

When readiness is absent, guidance passes without effect. When it is present, even partially, guidance aligns with it and gives direction to what would otherwise remain unformed. It does not impose direction. It confirms it.

Telemachus begins to act. He speaks within the house. He calls those within it to account. He does not yet restore order. He does not yet alter the condition. He moves. This is sufficient.

He departs. He leaves the house that has formed him and enters a field that is not his own. He listens. He sees. He returns. What has changed is not the condition alone. The man has altered his relation to it.

This is readiness.

It is not knowledge. It is not certainty. It is not the possession of a plan that guarantees outcome. It is the point at which a man can no longer remain as he has been.

From this, something becomes clear. A man cannot be formed from the outside. He may be directed, corrected, or instructed, but none of these produce readiness. They may accompany it. They do not create it.

The work does not present a method. It presents a relation.

A man is ready.

Another meets him.

The alignment occurs.

The movement follows.

Guidance does not impose. It aligns. The man moves. The guidance withdraws. The movement continues.

That is enough.

Chapter 19
What a Mentor Is and Is Not

The relation between men that the work presents is not one of instruction alone. It is not the transfer of knowledge from one who has to one who lacks, nor the imposition of form upon another, nor the shaping of a man according to an external design. These may appear within the relation, but they do not define it. What is shown is more exact.

A man stands within a condition he has not yet entered. He sees what is before him. He hears what is said. He recognizes disorder, but does not yet act within it. He remains where he is. The condition holds. Another appears. He does not replace the man. He does not act in his place. He does not remove the condition that stands before him. He speaks, and in speaking, he directs the man's attention to what he already sees. Nothing more is required.

This is the beginning of mentorship. It does not begin with instruction. It begins with alignment.

The mentor does not create readiness. He meets it. He recognizes what has already formed within the man and brings it forward into action. He does not impose what is not present. He does not extend beyond what the man can bear. He does not speak to what the man cannot yet receive. When he does, the words do not hold. They are heard, but they do not move the man.

Authority does not produce movement. Recognition does.

The sequence remains clear. A man sees and does not act. A man sees again and cannot remain. Another meets him, and he moves. The difference is not in what is seen. It is in what is borne.

The mentor does not stand between the man and the condition. He stands beside it. He does not remove difficulty. He reveals it. If he removes it, the man does not enter the condition. He remains outside it, unchanged. What appears as help becomes obstruction. What appears as guidance prevents movement.

The mentor does not protect the man from consequence. He allows it. This is not neglect. It is proportion. A man who is shielded from consequence does not learn to carry himself within it. He does not see what follows from what he does. He remains dependent upon the presence of another. The mentor does not establish this dependency. He removes it.

The mentor does not produce a likeness of himself. He does not create another who thinks as he thinks, speaks as he speaks, or acts as he acts. He does not reproduce his own form. He brings forward the man before him. The work does not present imitation as the aim. It presents recognition. A man who *imitates* acts according to another. A man who *recognizes* acts according to himself. The mentor directs the man toward the second.

This does not occur through instruction alone. Instruction may accompany it. It may clarify what is already seen. It may name what has appeared. It does not produce the movement. The movement arises when the man cannot remain as he has been. The mentor meets him there.

From this, something becomes clear. A man cannot be formed from the outside. He may be directed, corrected, or instructed, but none of these produce readiness. They may accompany it. They may align with it. They do not create it. The work does not present a method. It presents a relation.

> A man is ready.
> Another meets him.
> The alignment occurs.
> The movement follows.

A mentor appears. He does not impose. He aligns. The man moves. The mentor withdraws. The movement continues.
That is enough.

Chapter 20
The Return to the Reader

The movement that has been traced does not end within the work. It returns.

The reader has stood, for a time, within a different position. He has not been asked to adopt it permanently, nor to abandon what he has brought with him. He has been asked only to receive what is presented before seeking to explain it, to observe what is done and what follows from it, and to allow recognition to occur without being directed toward it. This has been sufficient.

What has been shown does not require extension. The works have remained where they are. They have not been altered, and nothing has been added to them. The difference lies in the position from which they have been encountered. The reader may now move.

He may return to the habits with which he began. He may resume analysis, comparison, and interpretation. He may place the work within its historical setting, examine its structure, and relate it to other works and ideas. Nothing in this is lost.

But something has been recovered.

The reader has seen what occurs when a man stands within a condition he cannot avoid, and how he bears himself within it. He has seen what occurs when a man moves through conditions that do not remain, and how he maintains alignment across them. He has seen what is revealed when order is abandoned and what is required to restore it. He has seen what it means to hold when one cannot move, and what it means to remain when one must. He has seen this without instruction.

From this, something becomes available that was not available before — not because it was absent, but because it had not been placed where it could be seen.

The reader may now encounter other works differently. He may observe conduct before seeking meaning, attend to sequence before drawing conclusion, and see what holds and what fails without requiring it to be named in advance. He may recognize patterns that do not depend upon explanation. This is not a method. It is a position.

The same holds beyond the page. The reader may encounter conditions that do not resolve at once. He may see actions that carry consequence beyond their moment. He may observe alignment, or its absence, in what is done. He may recognize without needing to interpret.

Nothing in this requires application.

The reader is not asked to carry these works outward as instruction, nor to impose them upon what he encounters. He is not asked to make them useful. He is not asked to draw from them a rule by which he must act. He is free to leave them where they are.

And yet, something remains.

He has seen that action does not stand apart from consequence, that speech binds and silence carries weight, that conduct is revealed under pressure, and that what is held within a man appears when it is met. He has seen that order does not persist where measure is abandoned, and that it does not restore itself without action. He has seen that movement does not require dissolution, and that holding does not require stillness. These are not conclusions. They are recognitions.

The reader may now stand again where he began.

But he does not stand in the same way.

Nothing has been added. Nothing has been removed. The works remain.

The reader has moved.

That is enough.

Sources and Notes

A. Primary Texts

The analysis in this work rests primarily on standard English translations of *The Iliad* and *The Odyssey*. No single translation is definitive. Each reflects choices of tone, diction, and emphasis that shape how the work is received. For this reason, multiple translations were consulted in parallel, with attention given not only to accuracy, but to the preservation of clarity, proportion, and continuity of action.

Among modern translations, those of Robert Fitzgerald, Richmond Lattimore, E. V. Rieu, and Robert Fagles were particularly useful. Fitzgerald provides a balanced rendering that maintains readability without overstatement. Lattimore remains closest to the structure and cadence of the original Greek, preserving sequence with minimal interpretive influence. Rieu offers a clear prose version that allows the action to be seen without overlay. Fagles provides a strong sense of narrative force and emphasis, useful as a point of contrast, though at times more interpretive than this book requires.

Where differences of phrasing affected interpretation, preference was given to readings that preserved the sequence of action most directly and allowed the conduct of the characters to remain visible without amplification.

The aim throughout was not to privilege a single version, but to remain attentive to what is consistently present across them.

B. Greek Terms

Occasionally, a Greek term is referenced where its range of meaning cannot be fully carried by a single English word.

The most important instance is *polytropos* (πολύτροπος), used in the opening of *The Odyssey* to describe Odysseus. It is commonly rendered as "resourceful," "wily," or "of many ways." Such translations tend to reduce the term to a trait. The original carries a broader sense of movement and adaptability across changing conditions. The phrase "a man of many turns" is used here to preserve that sense without importing modern psychological language.

A second term, *xenia* (ξενία), refers to the structured relation between host and guest. It is often translated as "hospitality," but the term carries a stronger sense of order, obligation, and proportion. It governs how a stranger is received, how he is treated, and how he, in turn, must conduct himself once received. In this work, the term is used not as a cultural detail alone, but as a model for how a work itself is to be received.

No further technical vocabulary is required. This book is presented so that it may be seen without dependence on specialized terms.

C. Classical Context

The question of how these works shape those who encounter them is not new. It appears explicitly in the writings of Plato and Aristotle, who considered the formative power of poetry and its effect on character.

Only those elements directly relevant to this question have been considered here. The purpose is not to engage in philosophical comparison, but to note that the concern with how a work forms the one who receives it belongs to the earliest reflections on these texts.

D. Oral Tradition

Modern understanding of the formation of these works has been shaped in part by the research of Milman Parry and Albert

Lord, whose studies of oral poetry demonstrated how long narrative compositions could be preserved, adapted, and transmitted without written fixation.

Their work provides context for understanding how these poems may have functioned when first heard: not as fixed texts, but as performed sequences carried by memory and shaped by use.

This context supports, but does not determine, the approach taken here.

E. Modern Orientation

Lectures and commentary by contemporary classicists — particularly Elizabeth Vandiver — have been valuable in clarifying historical setting, narrative structure, and the conventions of ancient reception. Such work provides orientation within the field.

Where this book differs is in emphasis. The present work does not aim to analyze these texts, but to restore the conditions under which they may be properly received.

F. Notes on Approach

This work does not proceed by argument, nor does it rely on secondary interpretation to establish its claims. It remains with the primary texts and attends to what is said and done within them.

Where references are made, they are offered not as authorities to be deferred to, but as points of orientation for readers who wish to explore further.

The reader is not required to consult them.

Final Note

These works do not depend upon commentary for their force. They require only that they be received in order.

If the position of the reader is restored, the need for explanation diminishes.

That is sufficient.